CLOUGH DYKE
WISTOW

Cawood Marsh Nov

CLOUGH DYKE WISTOW

A WINDOW ON NATURE

Writings and Illustrations
by
Alwyn Doyle

Water vole

William Sessions Limited
York, England

ISBN 978-1-85072-382-0

Printed in 11 point Plantin Typeface
by Sessions of York
The Ebor Press
York, England

To my parents, for nature and nurture. In memory of Edna, my late wife;
and to Kay, each for their love and encouragement.
To walkers and those who enjoy nature and our countryside.

'Nature never did betray the heart that loved her.'
William Wordsworth, 1798

ACKNOWLEDGEMENTS

For permission to reproduce the poems by John Clare from Curtis Brown Group Ltd,
London, on behalf of Eric Robinson. Copyright © Eric Robinson 1967.

For permission to reproduce the poems of Walter de la Mare from
The Literary Trustees of Walter de la Mare and the
Society of Authors as their representative.

For permission to reproduce the poem "Leisure" by the executors of the
W.H. Davies Estate and Jonathan Cape Ltd as publishers from the
Complete Poems of W.H. Davies.

My thanks to Maureen Williams, writer, for her careful checking of the text and
helpful suggestions, and to those who kindly gave permission to use my
paintings in their possession for reproduction. And, not least, my
thanks to the publishers of the poems.

The artist – Wistow Clough, August 1981.

River Ouse

Wolsey walk
to Cawood

Pump
house

Wolsey walk
to Wistow ▷

Wistow
Clough

Little
Steads

North dyke

Marsh Lane

Wistow Clough

INTRODUCTION

As I was sketching, the sudden rustling of a small creature forcing its way through tall grasses broke the stillness of a perfect summer's day. In a flash, two hares materialised just feet away. They paused in the open space between us, then dashed into the cornfield on my right; a few seconds later one returned and approached in short hops, stopping momentarily to nibble grass, eyeing me throughout, until I thought it would reach my feet. The hare's staring eye, twitching nostrils and breathing held me as I sat rooted, scarcely drew breath or blinked an eye. It was a moment to soak in. As though the hare satisfied all was well, turned and hopped back into the cornfield. It was this kind of experience of surprise and wonder, which held my attention at Wistow Clough for a long time. The location of Wistow Clough* with its dyke is off Marsh Lane, a short distance from the village of Wistow which is less than two miles North of Selby in N. Yorkshire.

I first came here after my son told me he would like to fish at the pond. We came a number of times and having an aversion to baiting and hooking a struggling fish, I found plenty to interest me otherwise. We found it to be a place, quite close, in the flat land of the Vale of York surrounded by farmland, with no outstanding features beyond a pond and a long, quite deep, wide dyke, with the river Ouse nearby. Yet I chose this place to carry out drawings, paintings, and write comments about nature in land devoted to farming. So much is focussed on aspects of wildlife in special places such as a nature reserve. This is working land where wildlife has retreated, and thrives, in the ribbons of land bordering the fields. A microcosm of nature.

Surrounded by many acres of fields, more than a mile to the nearest B road, there was peace and relative isolation, a haven, and these conditions helped me to dwell on the animal and plant life. What I discovered drew me back frequently for quite a long time in a spirit of serendipity, and this was best done alone with time to linger and make discoveries. The land although flat and apparently uninteresting takes on another dimension in the part known as Wistow Clough. The dyke's zigzag course straightens out before heading for the pond crowned by its tall brick pump house. This main dyke gathers water from numerous tributaries draining the many acres of land into the pond from where excess water is pumped into the Ouse. The river is flanked by a very substantial flood bank giving commanding views all around, and on a breezy day the willows clinging to the banks toss their slender fronds in ceaseless motion. Along here a public footpath, named after Cardinal Wolsey, connects the villages of Cawood and Wistow.

Most of the time I spent prospecting for plants or any feature catching my eye; other times I settled down to drawing or painting, and enjoying a sense of freedom and tranquillity coming from the countryside.

The comments and illustrations are a record of what I experienced throughout a number of years of the months of the year. During this time I was reminded of the patience needed, and again, the necessity of keeping still. The rewards of watching a hare hopping towards you, apparently unaware of your presence is a breathtaking and

---

* Clough is pronounced clew.

rewarding experience; one day I was surprised and delighted to watch a cuckoo fly directly to a branch near my shoulder. I studied it as closely as one might a bird in the zoo – this was wild and all the more real, what a regal waistcoat he wore!

I enjoyed this time immensely and the weather added a great deal as I became more in tune and adapted to its moods and, from flat land, we are led to gaze upward where ever changing clouds formations stimulate the imagination, and on clear sunny days, to its incomparable intensity of blue.

JANUARY

Little Steads

JANUARY

New Year's Day, 1984

A visit to the River Ouse and the dykes with a friend on a cold unsettled day. A biting wind plucked our clothing as we watched a kestrel poised against the sky looking for prey. With head into wind, he balanced with stiffened wings, like a high wire performer, then banked away to rise again above a more profitable spot.

At this point of the river bank there is a stand of willows planted by the river authority; their roots bind the soil and prevent erosion to the outside curve of the river bank. Last year I had been surprised to find the whippy growth cut almost to ground level, then realised this was to control growth. However, it would be at least two to three years before a former feeding ground of blue-tits and reed buntings was restored. At the same time, herbicides had been used to eradicate the splendid beds of stinging nettles. The demise of these plants had denied a birthplace for the larvae of the small tortoiseshell butterflies which normally thrive here. It is also a feeding place for the peacock and red admiral butterflies.

The dykes are perennially neat and close shorn after the late summer cut of the previous year. The shallow water is clear, corrugated by frequent winds; and the innocuous perfection of the banks belie the procession of flowers with their attendant insects which flourish throughout the spring and summer months.

Wistow Clou

9th January, 1984

I always arrive at the dykes with a feeling of anticipation and pleasure; today I was greeted by a magnificent rainbow which lent an aura of magic to the broad landscape. I noticed a group of fisherman's vehicles near the road leading to the pond and decided to walk the north dyke where I expected the wild life to be undisturbed.

The open fields were scoured by cold, tireless winds. Near the dyke, a large brown bird started up; through binoculars clearly saw the rhythmical beat of his wings as he melted into the landscape. Here was something new and interesting; hoping for another glimpse I moved forward and, twice, disturbed the bird. Each time it flew only a few inches above the brown furrows and then vanished; the vanishing trick was achieved through his perfect camouflage. When I moved again, he suddenly materialised soaring to approximately thirty feet, from whence it viewed me! I was now certain that I was looking at an owl. Through my field glasses, the large head and long barred wings with rounded tips helped me to identify him; he presented a spectacular image of brown and grey patterns. I based my impression that he was a short-eared owl on the fact that it was daylight when they usually hunt. In four years, this is only the second time I have seen an owl here.

11th January, 1984

I returned to the same spot, hoping I could find out more about the owls of this area. A strong wind brushed deep furrows across the water of the dyke. From the green shoots of winter corn, a flock of twittering skylarks rose as one, then swept to earth again for food and shelter. I found no owls and returned to my car feeling a little disappointed. However, I realised that patience is a virtue in observing wildlife.

Whilst sitting in my car over a warming cup of flask coffee, a sharp movement ahead caught my attention; it was just the merest flick of a pointed wingtip, and winging its way into the trough of the dyke, a kestrel hawk alighted in front of me. This was a brown speckled bird denoting a female, in contrast to the brighter coloured male. She dived towards the honeycomb of burrows on the opposite bank in a strike for a water vole; she returned without prey, and finally, springing from the grass with a few powerful strokes of wing, coursed the higher reaches.

The effectiveness of natural camouflage never ceases to catch me out. In this case I knew exactly where the bird was standing and yet, due to its blending perfectly with the background, I often lost sight of it. The ability to be inconspicuous is important to the female for her own sake as well as for her nest and young, particularly if the nest is on the ground.

11th January, 1982

The River Wharfe joining the river Ouse had burst its banks, flooding land around the dykes to a distance of approximately three miles to the south; then came ice which stilled the waters. My wife had made sandwiches and filled a flask with soup before setting off for a walk along a raised floodbank – and I wondered if we would reach the dykes.

Before long we were gazing across a frozen waste, broken only by the dark outlines of ancient trees and marooned farm buildings. The only visible sign of bird life consisted of a large flock of black-headed gulls standing motionless as though frozen to the ice.

Flooded field under ice

The vast whiteness, stretching to the horizon, was impressive and only an occasional surprising creak from the ice disturbed the pervasive silence. It was a comatose countryside and after two hours slow progress: unable to endure the penetrating cold longer, we retreated.

Some days passed before there was a reprieve; a slight thaw, and a slow recession of water, which enabled me to reach the dykes by road.

23rd January, 1982

I stopped the car where the road was shining with ice and gingerly made progress on foot to the dyke. I took photographs of the landscape, looking for the effects of silhouettes etched against light which I felt might express this hard winter.

Dozens of starlings and a scattering of fieldfares moved across the ice searching for food and I wondered if they were devouring the winter gnats which mysteriously appear during a warm spell. On a island by the roadside I found the bodies of three brown rats. Perhaps the extensive flooding and maybe lack of food had been too much even for these good swimmers.

High in a tree in a corn bunting appeared, reminding me of warmer days. The sun caught the ice and sent up blinding rays of light contrasting sharply with dark trees and tired herbage. I found that the normal water level had risen to inundate a small bridge and dyke completely. The surface was a swirling mass racing towards the pond. I wondered how the water-voles, normally living in burrows along the dyke, had reacted to this invasion. I could only imagine that they had retreated to higher ground where their survival would depend on digging fresh burrows. The fields, mute and eerie, showed paw prints in the snow as hares and smaller animals had moved in search of food and shelter.

In spite of the wintry scene, minute red buds of the hawthorn and green buds of the wild rose were emerging. My thoughts turned from the harshness of winter to the promise of colours of Spring.

23rd January, 1985

The long period of snow and extremely cold weather, together with mist and poor lighting, had deterred me from going into the country. Today was clear and sunny. I set off, hopeful of seeing something of interest. Through the binoculars, I was treated to a fine display of hover flying by a kestrel (sometimes known as windhover) as I watched him, I was surprised by the sudden appearance of a mature heron which flew across my line of vision within about six feet of the ground. A truly captivating bird with a body and wings in tones of black, white, and grey; the neck tucked will into his body prescribing graceful curve; and flying majestically with a steady beat of large, rounded wings.

Heron landing

I collected a stem of burdock (sticky-buds) for painting; this is a common plant in this area. Seeds are distributed by contact, the hooks on the outside edge of the seedhead cling when brushed by a passing object (an animal or human) and later are brushed off or fall to the ground. As small children, we collected these to throw at one another for fun as they readily stuck to your clothing.

At a distance I noted a showy magpie, one of quite a fair number nesting in the area. I have greatly admired this bird since the time, in early years at secondary school, when I spent part of my summer holidays on a farm. This was a high spot in my life, and I suspect, a time when my enjoyment of the countryside developed. One of my treasures of these years was the tail feathers of a magpie given to me by a farmer; I was fascinated by the sheer beauty of the iridescent colours emanating from an otherwise black feather – being a 'townie' this was magical.

Magpies

Fieldfares were still foraging before their migratory flight to northern Europe. The hawthorns and wild rose stripped of fruit were evidence of the diet of these and others of the thrush family.

25th January, 1984

After a fall of snow, I decided it would be a good time to look for paw prints and, if possible, trace the owners. The afternoon sun had changed in colour to faded orange, tinting the snow pale cream and rendering the shadows blue-grey. The branches of hawthorns and young ash in the hedgerows formed delicate tracery on the mantle of snow. My footfalls, crunching through the snow crust, were audible to creatures a field or two away, and I moved slowly to minimise sound. Disturbed patches of snow were clearly evident; the tell-tale marks of cavorting hares. Their trails were quite easy to pick up as individuals had moved from field to field; there were smaller prints on land near the dyke which I assumed would be those of the vole. I saw two hares which, resembling small terriers, loped across the whiteness towards the protection of a large tree stump.

An oystercatcher burst into flight close by; this was one of a number seen over the years and proves that this species is extending it's range from the seashore and estuary. I was attracted to the sound of whirring wings as a pair of red-legged partridges landed on nearby furrows. As I focused my binoculars on them they ran towards me with a wobbly clockwork motion and I was treated to a wonderful close-up of the exquisite patters of their plumage.

I was driven away by the intense cold and crunched my way back to Clough dyke; here I photographed the leaden fields in the retreating light. In the dyke, the ice was covered by a sprinkling of snow streaked with marks like those drawn on a steamy window pane. Against the flat greying sky to the north, two short-eared owls progressed on silent wings, their movement emphasising the stillness below. I felt great pleasure in watching their steady, meandering, graceful flight. Each complemented the other's movement, like cocks and horses at the fairground. On Little Steads a group of mysterious dots at a distance proved to be a party of hares, a dozen of them, mostly in pairs, and I realised that in a few weeks they would perform their ritual courtship.

Red legged partridge

As I left, the appearance of a fieldfare, displaying a boldly speckled chest and white flashes of the underwing, enlivened a brooding landscape.

26th January, 1985

Again, I was greeted by a white, tranquil landscape. I was soon rewarded, as a heron took off from the pond; he flew with his head into a stiff cold wind, only a few feet above the snow. This is a flying technique I had noticed before and I wondered if this was the same bird; was it to gain more lift from air blowing more swiftly nearer the ground? Was it for better camouflage, or was it an attempt to spot it's prey more easily where food at the pond had been in short supply?

A tawny owl, fieldfares and hares were out and about searching for food on this bitterly cold day. Near the riverbank, Water Board workers had stacked large bundles of willow branches in readiness for repairs to the eroding riverbank. I had learnt from one worker that these branches were cut from willows growing at various points along the bank. In strengthening the weakened bank, bundles are manhandled to make a "mattress" which becomes embedded in the silt, and are further fastened with stakes and ties. Well within a year, the branches have formed roots and a young stand of willows emerges. This is to the good for wildlife, particularly the reed-bunting and blue-tit which haunt this habitat; the willows too, are pleasing to the eye in their graceful drifts along the bank.

WINTER

Old January clad in crispy rime
Comes hirpling★ on and often makes a stand
The hasty snowstorms neer disturbs his time
He mends no pace but beats his dithering hand
And February like a timid maid
Smiling and sorrowing follows in his train
Huddled in cloak of mirey road afraid
She hastens on to greet her home again
Then March the prophetess by storms inspired
Gazes in rapture on the troubled sky
And then in headlong fury madly fired
She bids the hailstorm boil and hurry bye
Yet neath the blackest cloud a sunbeam flings
Its cheering promise of returning Spring.

From: Selected Poems and Prose of John Clare
Edited by Eric Robinson and Geoffrey Summerfield
Oxford University Press 1967
Ely House, London, W1

★ Hirple – to limp.

FEBRUARY

Track towards pump hou

FEBRUARY

5th February, 1984

Near the north dyke, a group of feral pigeons pecked it's way across a field, whilst overhead, a flock of greenfinches flew in characteristically jerky flight, up-down, up-down. Whilst taking stock of my surroundings, a strange bird appeared, flying close to the ground, straight as an arrow. I was surprised and excited at the prospect of discovering another species. The long pointed, rapidly beating wings were strange to me; I was impressed by the ease with which the bird flew over rising ground and sparse hedges, like a steeplechaser. I felt that this was surely the performance of a sparrowhawk; not for him the patience of the hovering, waiting kestrel, but a flashing, accelerated flight, calculated to take his prey completely by surprise. I was reminded of the time I watched a sparrowhawk plummet towards a housesparrow within a few yards of me; I had appeared at a crucial moment and it was difficult to tell which of the three of us was most surprised. The attacker quickly disappeared, leaving unharmed a very startled sparrow, and leaving me with a breathtaking image of a sparrowhawk with it's wings, legs and talons fully extended poised for the kill.

5th February, 1985

I have been to the north dyke on two recent occasions to complete the background to a painting of the oak gall and have found it to be a feeding ground of the short-eared owl. The first time there was one pair, but on the second visit there were two pairs and a single bird. I took this to be a fair indication of an ample food supply. They were truly magnificent birds with a wing span which I estimate to be at least three feet. They have remarkable patience in waiting for food and where I have found it impossible to find a water vole, the owl has succeeded. It seems that these owls regard me as harmless for they make no attempt to fly more than a few hundred yards, then settle. Through my glasses I distinctly identified the small 'ear' tufts, which of course, are simply feathers. I stayed long enough to do my work and left to give the birds a better chance of hunting.

8th February, 1983

I was pleased with publicity given to water colours of common wild plants I had exhibited. This, I hoped would draw attention to plants which often grow within crevices of concrete, the base of a wall and almost anywhere where there is sufficient soil, powerful enough to bore their way to daylight through hardcore and tarmac pavements.

11th February, 1985

I set out to the north dyke hoping to photograph an owl in flight. However, I only saw one, which was out of range, but an opportunity for photography was presented when a hare ran within a few yards. As it did so, I thought how compact a creature it looks from the front, compared with the side view. As I followed the field I counted at least sixteen overgrown stumps of what must have been a fine row of mature trees and I realised that, buried under the unkempt dried grasses was the knarled remains of a hawthorn hedge. I walked along the margins of the next field and found to my pleasure

Oak apples and North dyke

a different picture, for here a number of trees had been retained. The trees are a haven for wildlife, giving shelter also to humans and animals and, of course, provide an attractive landscape.

26th February, 1981

The wind had dropped and I followed the northern dyke finding little of interest. Fresh mole hills had formed on the banks and, embedded in the crumbly soil mounds, I discovered tiny snail shells. I accidentally flushed a splendid cock pheasant, the first I have seen here, although their tracks have been noticeable in the snow. A fine hare, displaying his shining white ears, tipped dark brown ran across a field of winter corn, his dark brown and white tail flashing. His rather bright, light brown coat was enriched with a darker patch of brown along his spine. I am still on the lookout for the courtship display of these wonderful animals. I found minute wisps of hare's fur caught on the soil, evidence perhaps of a chase or fight? The fur felt softer and warmer than cashmere – a perfect protection against the harshest weather. At the pond side the conspicuous nests of the magpies (with twigs clustered like iron filings to a magnet) are enclosed by a fortification of the spikey hawthorn branches. The nests are of dome construction which conceals the striking black and white feathers of the female whilst she incubates the eggs.

Cow parsley, dandelion, chickweed, coltsfoot, cuckoo pint and cleavers were beginning to show their first leaves in miniature amongst the young grasses. Land drains feeding the dykes poured out their quiet accompaniment to the promise of spring.

THAW

Over the land freckled with snow half-thawed
The speculating rooks at their nests cawed
And saw from elm-tops, delicate as flowers of grass,
What we below could not see, Winter pass.

by Edward Thomas
from: Palgrave's Golden Treasury
by J Press 1964

Towards Cawood Marshes

18

MARCH

Overlooking Little Steads

MARCH

6th March, 1984

The first sign of real warmth in Spring; a windless day when sound carries easily; bird life was plentiful and the insistent skylarks provided the solo performance as fresh as spring itself. There was constant movement in the sky as feral pigeons, wood pigeons, rooks, crows and magpies flew to and fro in search of food. It is time also of pairing up and nest building.

Attracted by the sight of two pheasants, I stopped by a small wood to look at the trees. Their branches were sharpened by the sparkling light and shade and the pendulous yellow catkins of the hazel glowed against the sombre colours of bare trees. The pheasants melted into the herbage and I was glad that here was another, although small, wild place providing shelter for plants and animals. From amongst the topmost branches, the clear, silvery notes of the robin constantly reminded intruders of his territorial claims.

This still woodland, bathed in the soft light of a weak sun, had an ambience of magic which can only be experienced first hand. It's secrets are found in the blending of black and sepia boles, branches, twigs and yellow catkins, the faded ochre grasses, a warm gleam of dull copper in tousled bracken, and a silence, broken only by a robin's trilling song. A small magical world.

We could think of March as the tail end of winter and it's apparent drabness, yet it is possible to find a sombre beauty in the countryside at this time. A distance away near the main dyke, a yellow hammer, besporting a saffron waistcoat, emitted a single, oft repeated note, echoing another of its kind nearby.

8th March, 1981

Clough Dyke on a cold day with a stiff westerly wind, but with some sun and patches of blue sky. I photographed the dyke facing east, for reference and then walked to the river. From the top of the flood bank I was greeted by an impressive view of very high water racing towards the river Humber and finally the sea. This huge volume of water is the culmination of spring rains and the contribution of distant tributaries in the Dales.

The fields were deserted, except for parties of foraging rooks, and above, an occasional scavenging blackheaded gull sweeping the river's course. I made my way back to the welcome protection of hawthorn and collected a spikey twig for painting; next time I must wear leather gardening gloves! As I trudged back over the margins of the wet, sticky warp* land I was grateful for my old fell boots. I photographed the dyke looking west, and also margins of the pond.

12th March, 1981

Late afternoon – following a week of milder weather, with a grey rainy sky and misty atmosphere. Earlier rains have helped the plants, and the dyke banks are bright green

---

* Flooded land with a deposit of fertile soil.

Ash and Common Reed

and lush. I made the visit short and collected flowers of dandelion and coltsfoot; coltsfoot was once an apothecary's herb used for easing coughs. As I walked back in the driving rain I realised the importance of moisture to slugs and snails. They were everywhere, clinging to stems and leaves and I discovered that the breathing hole in the black slug is in the mantle at the front.

13th March, 1981

A fine sunny day with cotton wool clouds (cumulus) moving against a clear blue background. The ubiquitous kestrel hovered into they eye of an easterly wind. It was coursing the main dyke in the hope of a meal. An apprehensive moorhen dashed for cover pattering across the water with its green webbed feet. I wondered if one day I would find a moorhen's nest.

Plants I found for identification by collecting the young leaves were the giant bell-flower, lady's smock (or cuckoo plant, and the food plant of the orange-tip butterfly larvae) meadowsweet, ribwort or ribgrass and meadow cranesbill. Meadowsweet has the properties of asprin whilst meadow cranesbill is one species of a large family, a familiar perennial to be found in our gardens which bears striking mauve blooms in profusion. I collected the dried seedheads of burdock for painting.

Lesser Celandine

16th March, 1982

The changing weather offered a sea of grey clouds and the surface of the dyke water trembled in the wind. My hands are chilled, but there was a feeling of spring which was warming to the soul, and the air has freshened. Trees are still naked, but amongst them the long stems of the wild rose are exposing sharp green tips of buds.

23

In a field to the north remnants of last season's sugar beet crop bear the teeth marks of the hare and vole; these scraps are as manna in the harshest winter. Along the uncultivated strips of land, the small thrusting shoots of January are flourishing – young, perfectly shaped plants, growing to the sound of trickling land drains. A covey of handsome redlegged partridges patrolled the fields, calling urgently.

17th March, 1982

The fickle March weather produced fine, bright conditions so I was able to paint outdoors, sheltered in my car whilst the persistent cold westerly howled around the windows.

I watched a pair of goldfinch threading their way through the wind and I was reminded once more of the amazing strength of a bird. There was no other wild life visible and the only real movement came from the endless rhythm of ripples caressing the surface of the dykes. The peacefulness came as a pause, as though nature held it's breath whilst spring waited in the wings. I painted for an hour, intending a return visit to complete the picture.

Hawthorn

23rd March, 1982

Excellent weather and at the dyke I looked for signs of a moorhen's nest without success. Warmed by the sun, midges danced in clouds above the banks on a windless day. Minnows flicked through the clear water, but I found no sign of frogs or toads. Apart from the presence of other fish in the pond the appearance of minnows confirms the condition of the water proving it to be sufficiently well-oxygenated for them to breed.

The cowslips in drifts were awakening with the appearance of their young leaves. Nothing of great interest caught my eye, however, the short period in the country was very refreshing and a reward in itself.

30th March, 1982

I bought a 1:50 000 O/S map published in 1979. I found some useful information of the area including tracks, footpaths and place names. Together with an O/S map of 1851 I had obtained earlier, I found the names Wistow Clough; clough meaning ravine or gorge; the fields to the south, Little Steads, stead meaning place or locality; the Nesses, where a former loop of the river Ouse had flowed, meaning a promontory or headland and Ing, wetland or marshland. Wistow Clough is to the south of an area named Cawood Marsh, and Marsh Lane, passing the Clough, indicate the early character of this piece of countryside, when in prehistoric times a huge marsh extended to the East coast of Yorkshire.

Black bird

A HARE

Eyes that glass fear, though fear on furtive foot
Track thee, in slumber bound;
Ears that whist danger, though wind sigh not,
Nor echo list a sound;
Heart.... Oh, what a hazard must thy wild life be,
With sapient Man for thy cold enemy!

Fleet scatterbrains, thou hast thine hours of peace
In pastures April-green,
Where the shrill skylark's raptures never cease,
And the clear dew englobes the white moon's beam.
All happiness God gave thee, albeit they foe
Roves Eden, as did Satan, long ago.

From: The Collected Poems
Of Walter De La Mare
Published by Faber & Faber in 1979

Alder-catkins

APRIL

Tops of the clouds

APRIL

1st April, 1984

March and April being months when hares are active, I came hoping to see something of their courtship rites. Through binoculars I found three hares intent on feeding from the young blades of grass and apparently ignoring my presence.

From the elevated position of the flood bank, my attention strayed to the carpet of fields spread before me. Some fields fringed by sparse hedging and knots of trees stretched for miles to the horizon; such is our flat land. On the field below, the hares continued eating, showing no desire to chase or 'box' in the manner of their courtship. The sun with a warmth sometimes surprising at this time of year, permeated and fused the scene into one of perfect tranquillity. This was reward in itself.

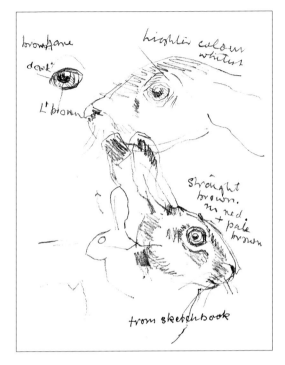

I was fortunate to be standing at one point behind a screen of young willows, when a large hare ran towards me and stopped a few feet away; sensing me, she loped away, but not before I had time to take in the colour and texture of her fur; her most arresting features were her large attentive, luminous eyes. It is at such a moment of contact with a wild animal, that, although you are a spectator, you also feel an intruder.

3rd April, 1980

I took my son to fish at the pond joining Clough dyke, whilst I tried out a pair of binoculars. On the river-bank, I watched a much magnified blue-tit, high in the willows methodically combing the catkins for food. The tits achieved this by prising open the divisions of the flowers in rapid succession; this is something I could not have seen without the aid of binoculars, a kestrel perched on the branch of an oak as he surveyed the land; I was able to appreciate the detail of his slender, tapering body ending in dark tail feathers. His wings are pale chestnut in the sunlight; his chest buff, evenly speckled; his short legs and yellow claws.

3rd April, 1982

Clough dyke:

Yellow hammers appeared in small groups, their yellow chest feathers bright in the sunlight; there were also a few linnets, rosy chested, quieter in colour but no less a joy to see; and there was a single corn bunting, distinctive enough with brown speckled

Kestrel

Bumble bee

32

feathers. It is good that the linnet enjoys a freedom denied in Victorian times when it was exploited for its delightful song and sold as a cage bird.

I was tempted to photograph a drift of celandines growing on the slopes. This was not an easy achievement with limited camera equipment; one simply had to adopt the attitude of a contortionist! I was lucky to retrieve my camera case which I discovered floating slowly downstream.

A peacock butterfly, roused from its winter hibernation, seeming to revel in the sun's warmth, flitted rapidly overhead. The occasional bumble bee droned by, one of which, seemingly magnetised by a small neat hole in the ground, disappeared within. I learnt that this could have been a queen bee either building a new nest or nurturing her young.

4th April, 1981

Easter Bank holiday Monday – a perfect day for the time of year; cloudy but bright with a fresh southerly wind. There were no fishermen at the pond leaving the main dyke to myself.

A scan of the slopes revealed that coltsfoot and cowslips were in bud with the promise of their clear colours when in full bloom. A pair of small birds proved to be blackcaps. These birds are visitors from the southern Mediterranean and extend their stay until October. At the pond margins, the hawthorn and wild rose were also in bud and at the opening of the dyke near the river, celandines scrambled over the slopes; nearby an incongruous clump of daffodils bloomed triumphantly, looking every inch the garden 'escape'.

Above the river, black headed gulls wheeled in their continuous quest for scraps of food. In the fields I saw yellow hammers; a bird which haunts the hedgerows of our country lanes. There were also a group of chiff-chaffs, arrivals from Africa. In the past, I have relied on the naked eye to observe wildlife and it was not until I made use of binoculars that I realised their value, especially for identifying small birds.

Peacock

5th April, 1981

A sunny day with clouds interspersed with patches of pale cobalt blue; colours in the landscape clear and fresh. This is when I feel good to be in the open, breathing fresh air, uplifting to the spirit.

Near the culvert off Marsh Lane, I found ground ivy with its small attractive purple flowers. Here too, are cow parsley, Lords-and-Ladies (cuckoo pint), dead nettle (already flowering) and daisy. All these plants are native, together with the creeping thistle which invades the herbage. The latter plant is a much loved source of nectar to a host of insects, including a number of butterfly species; of these, the small tortoiseshell is the commonest at Clough dyke.

As I walked along the dyke, I watched groups of the winter gnat in their yo-yo like dance movements (it is a gnat which does not bite humans!) The only movement on the water was caused by small, black water beetles (whirligigs). These creatures swim well and dive readily when alarmed; when diving they take with them an air supply in the form of a bubble encased in their wings.

This beetle also has the remarkable facility to see through two sets of eyes, above and below water. Through the clear water I watched a toad gently ease itself in reverse, into the silt and concealment.

7th April, 1981

On a short visit to Clough Dyke I noticed the stumps of reed stalks moving as though disturbed by what I could only guess to be a fish, and quite a large one. At close quarters I found myself staring at the cold eye of a large pike, possibly two feet in length. In front was a smaller pike. With an electrifying 180° twist of his body, the larger fish thrashed his way towards the pond, at one point leaping clear out of the water. The breeding season had started in February and I thought it possible that there was a male and female.

Small tortoiseshell

I took photographs of the river bank now brightened with lesser celandines, whilst above, an armada of snow-white clouds sailed in a sea of cobalt blue; each feature of the elements combined in a celebration of Spring.

30th April, 1984

I went to the riverside to paint from life; on my way photographing a small tortoiseshell butterfly which shone like a piece of fine enamelled jewellery. The soil on which it basked

Hedge sparrow's nest

was rich warp land, or river sediment, now showing deep cracks in a dry period; this crust emphasised the fragility of the butterfly.

My movements accidentally disturbed an ant's nest causing great consternation amongst the inhabitants. I watched in fascination as the ants set about a rapid repair of the object of their whole existence – the nest. I must be more careful!

Cowslip

SPRING

Now the slim almond tree
Tells April soon will be
Scattering her petals where
Snow still lies cold and bare.

Birds in its leafing boughs
Echoes of Spring arouse.
Piercing the drowsy earth,
Crocus her flower brings forth.

Wooing the bees. And soon
Winter's ice – silvered moon
Shall melt, shall kindle on high
Springtime within the sky.

From The Collected Poems
Of Walter De La Mare
Published by Faber and Faber, 1979

MAY

Meadow Cranesbill

MAY

1st May, 1984

A warm sunny spell continued and I went to the small wooded aread by the riverside to photograph butter-burr, now at it's best. The formation of the flowere head is not unlike that of a hyacinth and is delicately tinted cream and pinky-brown. At this stage, the leaves are almost insignificant and belie the later appearance of gigantic leaves resembling rhubarb leaves. It is said that the name "butter" burr is derived from a Victorian practice of wrapping butter in the leaves to retain it's coolness. I discovered a pair of small tortoiseshells about to mate, giving me a "double-image" – two jewels this time, painted bright by sunlight. I was inspired to photograph them.

Under the trees I found clumps of ramsons, thriving amongst the prolific bright green undergrowth. A lovely native plant, at home (along with the elegant Indian Balsam) in this shady, damp and cool area. The trees consist of alder, ash, hazel and black poplar and in their shelter amongst the upper branches, the nests of wood pigeons are woven.

This visit was curtailed by the early appearance of an elderly local farmer carrying a stick, and stiff with arthritis in one leg. Making a shrewd guess, he asked in a friendly manner "Are you a conservationist then?" I replied that I was interested in painting and photographing this part of the natural, uncultivated countryside, and added that I also enjoyed the walks. He defended the action of farmers in removing hedges "Some say we've left nothing for bird life" (which is true in certain cases!) Nodding towards the clump of hawthorns sheltering the pond, he said, "I reckon there are a few bits left, like yonder!" I thought of the bird life which, to my knowledge clings precariously to these trees for existence throughout the year. I did not argue, this man had been interested in profit and loss in farming all his life. He brightened as he gazed at a vast field of winter corn (which possibly had been divested of some hedging). Drawing his breath, "Now," he said, full of admiration for the ranks of bright green uniform blades, "we couldn't do that in t' owd days". All thoughts of wild life had vanished from his mind. He then tackled the subject of ramblers and couldn't see the sense of keeping a footpath open just for one walker each year. I did argue this point and said that "the law had not changed on the existence of footpaths, which now form a valuable part of what is becoming a scanty heritage in our countryside. People with more leisure will need to make greater use of the outdoors." I don't think that he agreed with this argument and our conversation dried up, signalling our departure.

3rd May, 1981

At Clough dyke I met cold winds and rain when I came on a short plant noting and collecting visit.

I found chickweed, common enough, but attractive with it's minute, white, starry flowers. Lady's smock (or cuckoo plant) vibrant with it's pink/lilac, deliciously scented, flowers and one of the food plants of the lovely orange-tipped butterfly. Low in the herbage lay the germander speedwell with it's tiny startling blue flowers with white centres. I also collected the common vetch, the hairy tare and garlic mustard; the odour of which is pungent when the leaves are crushed. The leaves, too, are edible eaten raw or

Ramsons

boiled. Splendid drifts of this plant are common along the river bank and ditches. I found the horse-tail in abundance and the wild rose scrambling happily among the sturdy branches of the old hawthorns, now in bud by the pond. I tested the tansy for the fine aroma of it's crushed leaves; this plant has been used in medicine and cookery. The brambles which eke out a living on the dyke banks are pruned to pigmy size, together with a few aspiring yellow willow saplings, by a mechanical bank trimmer which does the job of controlling the herbage along the dyke.

I collected a piece of meadow vetchling and noticed the ground elder (bishop's weed or goutweed) once used to treat gout. The leaves can also be used as spinach served with butter. The hogweed (or cow parsnip) once used as pig fodder is thriving, and these plants possess young shoots which may be eaten, tasting similar to asparagus.

I also noticed coltsfoot, whose flower (in the early stage of development) resembles the fetlock and hoof of a colt, like the butter-burr, the leaves develop fully, long after the flowers.

I left the dyke aware that Spring was here.

6th May, 1983

After days of rain, I turned out without a coat for the first time this year. The sun was warm and the sky filled with brilliant white clouds. Insects are lively in May and my

40

Lady's Smock

attempts to photograph the green veined butterfly and bumble bee went unrewarded. I watched the flight of a green veined butterfly and marvelled at the skill with which it dodged the wind in zigzag fashion. It flew a course in line with the grassy margin of a field. The distance of about two hundred yards was covered in perhaps two minutes.

Near the pond, I watched a handsome, grey wagtail; I carefully noted it's movements, hoping I would find a clue as to the whereabouts of it's nest, but my search went unrewarded.

7th May, 1983

Circling the pond, and peering into the darkness of the hawthorns, quite suddenly I found myself gazing at a tangle of dried reed leaves forming a platform for seven moorhen's eggs. Had the nest been concealed amidst the dense brambles below, I would not have seen it. This bird, however, in it's wisdom had built her nest in a junction of sturdy, prickly hawthorn branches, four feet above ground level, beyond the reach of predators. At first sight the eggs were not easy to see blending as they did with the light brown strands of the common reed. I gazed at the seven perfect shapes with a feeling of pleasure, a degree of awe, and a sense that I was an intruder.

Steep banks rise above the dykes, pond and river, and once more, I made an awkward descent to get a closer look and to photograph this treasure. I used an aperture setting of f2 at 1/15 sec. (ASA 64) and propped myself firmly against a tree trunk to obtain a sharp image. After disguising the nest with a broken branch, I retreated, feeling pleased at the prospect of developments. I covered my tracks through the long grass intending to return as soon as possible.

9th May, 1983

After a morning of incessant rain, the sun came out and I returned to the pond to make a quick drawing of the moorhen's nest. The bird had already slipped off the nest and was attempting to distract me by calling from the pond. I spent a few minutes developing a drawing I had started from memory, adding colour notes.

41

Moorhen's nest

In the fields nearby there was little evidence of other birds and I felt this could be due to the strong winds. I searched again for the grey wagtail's nest without success whilst over the pond the first swallows were feeding on the wing.

12th May, 1983

After more rain I went to the pond in the evening and approached this time from the south side. Once again, the moorhen sensed my approach and flew over the water as before. My "camouflage branch" had not been disturbed, but one egg was missing, which puzzled me. Incubation takes three weeks; I had discovered the nest six days ago, so allowing four or five days for the eggs to be laid, approximately eleven days had elapsed. It was possible that the eggs had been laid much earlier. Had one hatched and the chick left the nest, or had the egg been eaten by a predator? I thought that it was possible that the egg had been eaten, or that the chick had fallen out of the nest. I wondered if other eggs would suffer the same fate and decided to keep an eye on developments.

16th May, 1982

To the dyke to collect plants for pressing and identification. Collected – black medic, cow parsley, ground ivy, dandelion, cleavers, ladies smock and garlic mustard.

We have had little rain throughout April and plants are stunted. I watched the movement of small, fast moving spiders inhabiting the stones near the small ditch.

17th May, 1982

Very warm and humid, I watched the brown speckled butterflies flitting restlessly to and fro and, whilst I felt that most, if not all, are wall browns, I wondered if I might find, say, a small pearl bordered fritillary amongst them. They were moving so quickly it was difficult to know. I have noticed that the small tortoiseshell readily takes nectar from ground ivy.

At the mouth of the main dyke, entering the pond, hundreds of tadpoles wriggle to surface and descend to the depths. From a bed of common reed a moorhen hurled itself across the water and I wondered if the bed concealed a nest. I took photographs of the ground ivy, cleavers and birds foot trefoil. There were numerous bumble bees going about their business (in the genus – there are sixteen British Species).

Wall butterfly

Dog rose

18th May, 1983

Numerous showers had produced abundant growth in plants, creating an arena of fresh, bright green which gladdened the eye and refreshed the mind. Along the pond margins, the tall stinging nettles served as host to the blob-like protuberances of the common snail which fed undisturbed. I photographed one at shutter speed 1/125 sec. (1/250 sec. Would have been better, to compensate for the movement of playful breezes).

19th May, 1981

One of the best days of the year, bright and warm, and the dyke was be-decked with "Queen Anne's Lace" (cow parsley) with it's exquisite creamy flowers. A common plant, but when closely examined, is endowed with long elegant stems, terminating in the delicate tracery of cool green leaves. It is present everywhere – a reminder of spring.

Basking on the stones of the bridge were two wall brown butterflies which I photographed with an Instamatic camera. This common butterfly is beautifully marked and I always see it afresh.

I am seldom watched as I go about my walks, but today was an exception. I was scrutinised intently by a group of cows. From the top of the pond bank the first comers gazed with increasing curiosity, and they were soon joined by others, forming a solid body with the pond behind me. My line of retreat was cut off, however, I ignored the distracting snorts of indignation and concentrated on taking my picture. I soon heard the sounds of slithering hooves and tearing grass and was in time to see a large tossing head within a few feet of me; others followed suit. I gave a great shout and the effect rippled through the herd which obediently turned away – I was saved!

24th May, 1981

On my way to the dyke I noticed swallows alighting at the roadside to pick up beaksful of soft mud from the puddles. This forms the mortar to their nesting material of dead grasses.

Near the river, I saw my first orange-tipped butterfly; the fresh colours of the male contrast well with the spring greens of the herbage. I still wonder at the speed with which they flit over the fields.

On reaching the moorhen's nest, I found the female sitting until the last moment, when she departed noisily. From the safety of the water she gave a single regular warning note, I stayed only a few minutes in order to minimise the disturbance. It is eleven days since I first spotted the nest and I was relieved that she was still incubating. My twig screen was undisturbed, and the six eggs were intact! A few yards from the nest I discovered a dead moorhen chick. Perhaps this was the missing one? As I gazed at it's body, I detected a gentle regular movement, as though it was breathing. Was it alive? Then I noticed, underneath the body, a dark coloured beetle which appeared to be lifting the body on it's back. Also, on top of the carcase was another beetle with the orange/red and black markings of the burying beetle – this one appeared to be feeding.

Later, I saw the male grey wagtail again displaying his radiant yellow breast. The bright sunlight intensified clear colours and light tones, making the white flowers of garlic mustard shine like stars; there are splendid drifts of this plant in parts of Clough dyke.

Along the roadside I found greater stitchwort, resembling gypsophila, a bright, white, pretty flower and found this charming plant to be common along the lanes.

24th May, 1983

I went to the dyke with a local lepidopterist who was surprised at the variety of butterflies we saw. I looked in on the moorhen's nest and saw only three eggs. Hoping to find some young moorhens to photograph, I moved further down the slope and realised that there were also two fluffy black chicks in the nest. I became so engrossed in watching their movements that I lost my opportunity. Their mother made a low call from the water, and as though responding, the chicks carefully climbed out of the nest and vanished silently into dense brambles below. I was left to wonder at what appeared to be a simple and effective rapport.

May is a month of burgeoning flora and fauna, crowning the emerging life of early Spring.

25th May, 1984

I cycled out to collect a few specimens of ramsons for painting. A generous measure of sun and rain had nurtured well developed plants. On either side of the hedgerows fine crops of barley swayed in the northerly breezes. I passed well established bluebells, greater stitchwort, and drifts of dandelions (some already seeding), bright yellow buttercups and banks of tall grasses. To this collection, were added hogweed, cow parsley, stinging nettles and brambles.

As I approached the pond, a heron climbed steeply and flapped away over the river. I followed the river, passing willows filled with bird calls. I studied a male reed bunting through my glasses, admiring the fresh, contrasting, light and dark tone of his feathers.

Reed bunting

From the footpath along the floodbank I moved into a mysterious pattern of light and shade, and the eerie silence of the woodland. Here the sheltered grasses, Indian Balsam, butter-burr and beds of ramsons grew uninhibited, lush and erect where the rich, moist warp land nourishes them to the full. I collected a few stems of ramsons in bud, just enough to paint in the studio as the petals open.

I left as evening approached and walked along the raised floodbank westwards into the changing light of evening. From here I had an uninterrupted view of our flat landscape "pancake land!" To the south, a darkening wood hugged the land, in the distance, the glinting tower of Wistow parish church crowned the rooftops of the village. Nature in repose, ready for sleep. There was a timeless quality about the scene and I reflected on the age of buildings I knew in Wistow. I thought of the Victorians, and through history to the 8th and 9th centuries when Vikings sailed this river to land an army for its march to Stamford Bridge. Viking bones may well lie in this land for it was also from here that the remnants of the defeated army sailed back to Denmark. Quite recently, an unidentified ancient sword was found on the river bed in this area.

45

When I reached the dyke, I saw numerous pond skaters and below them swam thousands of tadpoles moving in a steady stream towards the pond; no doubt many of them would be devoured by predators lurking there.

I found that at this time of year, the yellow hammer was much in evidence, frequently seen perched high in the trees flanking the roadside.

SONNET – THE THRUSH'S NEST

Within a thick and spreading hawthorn bush
That overhung a molehill large and round,
I heard from morn to morn a merry thrush
Sing hymns to sunrise, and I drank the sound
With joy; and, often an intruding guest,
I watched her secret toils from day to day –
How true she warped the moss to form a nest,
And modelled it within with wood and clay;
And by and by, like heath-bells gilt with dew,
There lay her shining eggs, as bright as flowers,
Ink-spotted-over shells of greeny blue;
And there I witnessed in the sunny hours,
A brood of nature's minstrels chirp and fry,
Glad as that sunshine and the laughing sky.

By John Clare
From The Wood is Sweet – John Clare
Chosen by David Powell 1971
Published by Bodley Head

*From the rising ground of riverbank facing west, with pond flanked by
hawthorn and dyke snaking along in centre. Oil painting.*

JUNE

Summer – small dyke to the north.

JUNE

2nd June, 1981

An evening visit. Heavy rain earlier, had left the cart track to the river scattered with deep luminous puddles. I photographed cow parsley bordering the dyke and, in the water below, I discovered hundreds of tadpoles swimming away from predators living in the pond.

I photographed the northern dyke stretching to west and near the mouth of the pond where damsel flies flitted amongst the leaves of reedmace. The damselfly is often difficult to photograph due to it's unpredictable movements, when, at the point of shutter release, it flies away like a miniature helicopter.

Since I began identifying plants this year, I have noted almost forty species and today I added the marsh thistle; on inspection they prove even more distinctive than when I first noticed them.

3rd June, 1985

After weeks of indifferent weather, we have a spell of hot sunny weather. The rainy conditions have produced ample plant growth and the stalks of corn and barley are almost two feet high. There has been a change in the countryside, from the bright greens of Spring to a deeper colouring; the barley fields in a buff colour, the waving seed heads a pinkish russet in the sunlight. At the same time, the activities and sound of bird and animal life have slowed down and become quieter. Family life has taken over, the young are being nurtured and older offspring are already fending for themselves. Sounds of family groups of partridges hidden deep in the tall barley stalks seem like a strange language interspersed with frequent soft chuckling sounds, pleasant to the ear.

female Mallard

A female mallard burst into flight with rapid, laborious wing beats, from the spot where I had previously seen a drake resting. She came from a steep bank on North Dyke, where brambles made an impenetratable mass and created an ideal nesting place for them – a place quite inaccessible to me.

A pair of hares were playing in a large field of sugar beet, whilst another pair cropped the grasses bordering the field. Hare droppings littered these margins, clearly marking their feeding grounds, but there were no signs of their presence amongst the beet and no signs of beet leaves being eaten.

Scanning the field with my binoculars, I spotted a sitting lapwing, with it's partner standing close by, and I hoped this indicated a nest with eggs. I made a sketchy diagram of the spot for reference. During this time, I noticed a hare hop within inches of the sitting bird causing no alarm.

The banks of Clough Dyke were rich in herbage including the showy cream flowers of cow parsley and the white flowers of hedge garlic. Further down the star-like flowers of water crowfoot spangled the dark waters. Altogether a good time to be out looking at nature.

4th June, 1985

Lapwing's nest

Returned to find and photograph the lapwings nest. I located the female sitting, with her vigilant partner standing nearby. As I expected, the female left her scrape as I approached, hurrying away to distract me, whilst the male took to the air calling in alarm. He lined up for a dive, creating a whooshing sound as air was forced through his wing feathers. He gave a spectacular display of aerobatics as I moved towards the nest which I found quite easily by using the fixed points of my diagram. I felt the same thrill as I did as a schoolboy on finding four perfectly shaped, mottled eggs. Their colouring was excellent camouflage, very necessary in such a vulnerable position. The "scrape" (so called because the male literally scrapes out a shallow depression, around which the female places a few pieces of vegetation) is also invisible, except to the searching eye.

8th June, 1985

I came to see the developments at the lapwings next, thinking that the eggs might have hatched and this proved to be the case. My presence disturbed the birds and I was mobbed by four lapwings which enlivened the scene by their circling and diving and the uttering of urgent alarm calls. The distraction created becomes an accepted fact to anyone studying wildlife, and I retreated to the cover of some nearby elder shrubs. From this vantage point I scanned the beet field with binoculars, and detected to my surprise, the movements of chick lapwings. Like their parents, they foraged for insects, and I was soon aware of a greater number of both parents and chicks than I had originally thought inhabited the field. The chicks rely upon their natural camouflage of mottled down and their ability to conceal themselves until they are able to fly. Also their attentive parents attempt to distract interlopers at the first sign of danger. I had quite unwittingly put this system to the test when I made at least two attempts to approach the families. The chicks "melted away" and the protective adults flew about me in a whirling protesting mass. I have since heard from a bird-watcher that lapwing chicks lie perfectly still until the danger passes.

Young lapwings

12th June, 1985

At this time of year, the weather frequently lapses into cold winds from the north, as tonight. Long grasses swished like horses tails and bend double under the wind. The numerous hares feeding, did so with ears laid back to avoid the wind. They shared a field with three pairs of lapwings which accepted their presence, perhaps because their young are now fending for themselves. A group of partridge and skylarks had joined them, whilst diving swallows scooped a living from the air. Wildlife young and old thrived in the long early summer days of abundant food.

On the north dyke amongst the deep vegetation, the bright yellow flower of the stately, smooth hawksbeard caught my eye. It grew as a thread of yellow amidst the grasses. On the water the encroaching duckweed showed trails formed by feeding moorhens. There was no butterfly or moth to be seen, only midges and craneflies hovered over the grass in this cold weather.

A pair of yellowhammers were flying and perched at various points, one which carried a strand of grass made me suspect that they might be choosing a late nesting site. Yellowhammers are striking birds with outstanding, clear yellow feathers concentrated on head and chest.

15th June, 1984

This must surely have been the hottest day of the year at the North Dyke when I went along to work on a drawing. Near the small stone bridge where I worked was a purging blackthorn shrub. The soft, lulling, incessant hum of bees attracted my attention and I realised that the minute blossoms of the tree were swarming with these insects. The blackthorn is a native shrub whose berries ripen in September; when gathered they were at one time used to produce a strong purgative, or in a milder form; Syrup of Blackthorn. In the 1900's this shrub was also useful to the artist as Sap Green which was derived from the berries. The fruit also makes a useful dye, which is fixed with an alum mordant, the young fruit producing yellow, whilst the mature fruit yields a hue of green.

17th June, 1984

Another perfect hot day, when I went to the same place to complete my drawing in the idyllic setting of bridge, water, blossoming trees and fields of corn. Engrossed in my drawing, I was startled by the sound of rustling grass vigorously disturbed by an animal and I then saw two hares, which ran within a few inches of me, and disappeared noisily amongst the tall heavy-eared corn stalks. The larger of the two (which I took to be a doe) re-appeared sniffing, nostrils dilating rapidly, as she cautiously came towards me. The sniffing sound was surprisingly loud from such a relatively small creature. Behind this most salient defence of nose and nostrils was the most perfect specimen of a brown hare. I think that this was one of the most exciting encounters I have had with a wild animal; I tried to breathe lightly and willed myself to avoid blinking. She came nearer and paused to take a closer look; I thought it possible that she might even sniff my shoes, but she stopped to eat grass a yard away from me. I felt that I would never have another experience like this again as I studied the animal with as much ease as though it were tame. The loud sniffing continued, and when that staring eye was satisfied, she moved steadily away into the thick forest of stalks to join her mate. It had been a great experience and it was a few minutes before I resumed my drawing.

Before I left, I glanced at the water and noticed the hundreds of tadpoles larger that when I last saw them, and I thought about their survival ratio at this stage, and later as young frogs on land. Predators, pike, kestrel, owl and heron must surely relate to the quite small number of frogs which survive.

17th June, 1985

I found the lapwing families again, and noted how the female gathered her brood together, watching each one as it snuggled into her wing and breast feathers as she squatted. I realised that the sugar beet leaves would grow as the young increased in size, thus providing cover for feeding.

22nd June, 1983

A good day to be at Clough Dyke in early afternoon; it was really hot where the sloping sides of the dyke made a sun trap and I sweat as I moved along. The waist high vegetation was at it's best, and the grasses I photographed shed their seeds at a touch. Cow parsley, hogweed, sowthistle and hawkesbeard flowered magnificently. What a wonderful time of the year, very distinctive, with it's magical range of colour and texture in flowerheads and stems. Leaves and grasses were alive with busy insects each providing it's own accompaniment to the orchestra around me. And there was variety of movement from the different species, varying according to their feeding habits and the size and

Hare in cornfield

shape of their wings. A few inches above a plant, hoverflies had settled, others restlessly moved from flower to flower, and others droned off to distant blooms, whilst some crept and sprang from stalk to stalk. A few buzzed loudly, lingered in mid air for a few seconds then dropped amongst the petals. I found all this activity very entertaining.

24th June, 1985

After making a drawing of the landscape, I searched the fields of beet with binoculars and found that the young, who sixteen days earlier were only 2" to 3" tall, were now young adults, capable of flying. They proved this at my approach, and as they soared to thirty feet and gently landed I estimated over twenty individuals, I felt please to see so many birds successfully reared and grateful to have watched their progress. Four eggs per nest and assuming four nests and four pairs would total twenty four birds. Their usefulness to the farmer is easy to understand as they spend their feeding time combing the fields for insects. The lapwing is an elegant bird at rest, with iridescent dark colouring set in white areas. In flight he is an entertainer with a fine repertoire of breathtaking clownlike tricks especially during courtship and in the protection of his young.

28th June, 1981

A month of changeable weather, following on from two very wet months. No "flaming June" this year! The southern bank of Clough Dyke was a scene of lush herbage, stirred by the winds and warmed by the sun. There was a unique and familiar harmony of the elements, combined with growth. These are the qualities which lure one back during the seasons to savour them again and again.

Meadow Brown on Ox-eyed daisy

The unexpected also occurs in the countryside; today I was confronted by another "find" – at my feet was a moorhen (mere hen, hen of pond or lake, water-hen). It was dead, but in perfect condition, except that close examination showed curious pink areas on the crown of it's head where feathers were missing. I was mystified, but felt very lucky to be able to examine a bird in this way. Apart from the slight damage, it's feathers were perfect; it's undersides a quite dark and flawless grey with the handsome black back shading to a greenish bronze. The fine leaf green legs scaled like lizard skin; a reminder of it's reptilian ancestors 150 million years ago. Another wonder of nature. I buried it in the tallest herbage.

A fine specimen of hemlock blossomed a few yards away, a graceful miniature tree. This plant has a tall green stem splashed with purple slender branches crowned in clusters of creamy florets. However, it is poisonous and children should be warned not to touch it or the skin may become blistered. The banks of the north dyke happily protected from wind seemed like another world. Here the dyke is wide and forms a sun trap, causing heat to radiate from the grasses, which today reached above my waist. This hollow makes an ideal habitat for butterflies, moths and a multitude of insects and larvae. Some insects I recognised instantly; the male orange tipped butterfly, with it's deliciously coloured wing tip brightening the green grasses. The female of this species is simply cream and easily mistaken for the green veined butterfly. Everywhere, bumble bees sampled the nectar of the tufted vetch, the ox-eyed daisy and the meadowsweet which lined the dyke bank. There were pale green caterpillars and ladybirds; moths fluttered between the tall grass stems and two meadow brown butterflies joined the throng. I felt the vitality of this teeming life but there was also harmony and a great sense of peace. In the water below was another world of life which I have yet to discover.

I photographed an egg carrying spider, resting on a leaf of a spear thistle and I brought back a piece of the tufted vetch whose tendrils grow from the tip of it's leaves. This enables the plants to climb and garland the long grasses. My collection was completed with a piece each of the meadow vetchling and the branched burr reed, the latter being a fine plant for drawing, with it's delicate contrasting shapes.

Burr Reed

A SWALLOW

A sharp movement in the air,
His entrance. Rapid clipping strokes
Propel the way. Airborne food awaits,
Scooped into the gaping, short, bewhiskered beak.
A flight, well prescribed, guides his life.
Rising, swooping – a sheet of water gives arrow
Flight, skimming tight.
With a boundary, a sudden turn; on vibrating
Wings a towering climb of ease;
Hollows suck him in.
A wonder of feather and life twists and turns
In dancing pattern.
Seen and gone, leaving a memory of perfection,
Softly mocking counterfeit.

A.J.D.

JULY

Water vole   "Ratty"

JULY

1st July, 1981

Stayed at the dyke approximately one hour, when I noted or collected certain plants which thrive in damp conditions including the welted thistle, the common reed, the amphibious bisort, the bullrush (or reedmace), the water forget-me-not (also known as scorpion grass). This latter plant is recognised by the curving leaves branching on each side of the stem below the terminal flower. I also found yarrow (or milfoil) with its pinkish white flowerhead, comprised of a myriad florets, heavily scented with the smell of honey, and I discovered wall lettuce. It is unfortunate that the elegant yellow flag iris, which grows at a little distance by the roadside, does not flourish here.

7th July, 1981

There were drifts of Indian balsam (policeman's helmet), growing in the narrows of Clough dyke. This lovely stately plant, so much a lover of moist soil and much visited by bees, also grows freely along the river bank; it is an introduced annual, now naturalised. I have seen on close examination, the effect of sunlight shining through the flowerhead, rendering it a delicate pink transparent wonder. The native great willow herb or codlins (apple and cream), is just coming into flower. The red-vined dock, another native, grows sparsely in the vicinity and the great stalks and swollen joints of hogweed are very evident. The elegant hedge woundwort is flowering; as the name suggests, this plant was once used for healing wounds as it contains volatile oil with antiseptic properties.

It was a warm peaceful evening as I watched a few meadow browns seeming to play hide and seek between the tall grass stalks on the bank sides and I marvelled at their unerring flight.

This was my introduction to this butterfly and, as I watched one clinging to a stem, I saw the effect of the rather startling 'eye' which appears on the forewing; when this closes the insect seems to vanish into its surroundings.

At my feet I found the native plant, creeping cinquefoil, said to have been used by the Egyptians as a cure for malaria. Amongst the herbage I found the greater burnet saxifrage, another plant with medicinal properties, once used to ease colic and indigestion and also to dissipate kidney and bladder stones.

11th July, 1982

A splendid day of warm breezes with plenty of sunshine and the dyke looking at its best. There were many wall brown butterflies, small tortoiseshells and cabbage whites taking nectar from a variety of plants, a favourite one being the creeping thistle.

I felt that this is perhaps one of the best times of the year to study flora and fauna when they are most varied and prolific. Marguerites, yellow vetchling, meadowsweet and the giant bellflower were very evident and the yarrow, white dutch clover, vetch and field poppy added to the pageant.

The cuckoo also finds this place to its liking. As I admired one at close quarters, I appreciated his handsome appearance whilst reflecting on the roguish habit of the female to 'use' the nests of other birds as a nursery for her unruly and deadly offspring. I marvel that evolution guides the cuckoo chick's instinct for survival, to turf out the existing eggs one by one by wriggling them into a hollow area on its back, then tipping them over the edge of the nest to destruction. And as a huge bonus, thereafter, the chick is fed by the foster parent. Another remarkable fact is that the cuckoo's egg is capable of mimicry with a close match to the colouring of the host's eggs.

14th July, 1983

A remarkable week of hot weather and today the temperature was in the 90's. Although quite late in the evening, the stones of the bridge were still warm. It was windless and the sky was dappled with mackerel clouds. These clouds always appear to be distant, resembling lacy patterns; two feeding swifts cleaved the air high above on scimitar shaped wings. It was a classic summer evening, too seductive to miss for those who have time

Giant Bellflower

Heron

Joseph Doyle

to enjoy the countryside. Although the barley is now golden, the corn is still green. Gold and green, familiar and attractive colours in the patchwork of fields.

In Clough dyke, the sword-like, rich green leaves of the reedmace pierced the air; this is a perfect habitat for the moorhen which gently weaves a secret course between the dense sturdy stems. The surrounding banks of the north dyke are covered by a tall jungle of grasses, with meadowsweet dominating on one side and rosebay willow herb apposite. Amongst the tall stems of creeping thistle, colonies of small tortoiseshell larvae twitch as they feed; their early homes of grey webs hanging below. Where the grass has been trimmed by the tractor with motor cutters attached, the stubble hints of Autumn.

The setting sun was too bright to stare at and below the mackerel sky the colours changed to those of a sandy desert, suffused with rosy pinks. Along the footpath, I disturbed the resting meadow browns summoned to their haunts of the night; I found them using their forelegs to better effect than their hind ones, which often slipped.

15th July, 1981

I found the black medic in flower (the given name indicates the colour of the ripe seeds). Bird's foot trefoil was also in bloom, this name is associated with the shape and angle of the seed pods – sometimes three or four pods spread at right angles from the stalk. The names 'Bacon and Eggs' and 'Tom Thumb' are two of a great number of local names. Pineapple weed or pineapple mayweed, a member of the daisy family was also flowering; this is an introduced annual, possibly from America and is also known as kayless chamomile. It grows freely on waste ground and is easily recognised as a yellow 'button' flower without petals. The leaves when crushed give out a scent of pineapple. Ragwort, food plant of the cinnabar moth, was growing more sparsely. I collected a seed pod of cowslip to broadcast along the bankside and on counting the dark ripe seeds I found forty.

15th July, 1987

My walk along the river bank was in a warm, humid atmosphere. There had been many showers which gave a freshness to the herbage. The colours and tones of mother-of-pearl subtly shaded the sky; a light breeze produced a rhythmic swish and rustle of grasses creating a magical ambience; a small part of summer in a seductive mood.

My steps along the flood bank, (part of the Wolsey Walk) brought me to the towering poplars of the small woodland in full leaf, rich in greens. Of birds, I noted six species, four of butterflies and nineteen of plants each referred to in previous notes.

17th July, 1982

Along the pond margin, where the cattle shuffle down the steep grassy bank to drink, forget-me-not, brooklime, and celery leaved crowfoot grow freely. The bank of creeping thistles nearby attract the small tortoiseshell, which flit to and fro, feeding on nectar.

It is the season of 'thunderbugs' (with bodies slightly over 1 mm in length) which proliferate in the ears of corn and fill the air with their minute bodies and cause much irritation and tickling as they creep over one's skin.

26th July, 1982

Clough dyke was a perfect sun trap today, with no breezes. Cabbage whites, small tortoiseshells and peacocks flitted restlessly from flower to flower.

The lighting was good and the opportunity to photograph the pond was too good to miss. I chose the entrance of the dyke to the pond (now covered with reed and pondweed) as the subject. In the centre of the pond were grouped a dozen slow moving, shadowy shapes and, as they were approximately one foot in length, cigar-shaped and dull in colour, I identified them as young pike. Near the pond margins a moorhen, perturbed and protective, ferried her two chicks through the reeds. One could appreciate that in the absence of fishermen wildlife of the pond had gained in freedom.

THE SNAIL

All day shut fast in whorled retreat
You slumber where- no wild bird knows;
While on your rounded roof-tree beat
The petals of the rose.

The grasses sigh above your house;
Through drifts of darkest azure sweep
The sun-motes where the mosses drowse
That soothe your noonday sleep.

But when to ashes in the west
Those sun-fires die; and, silver, slim,
Eve, with moon upon her breast,
Smiles on the uplands.

Then, all your wreathed house astir,
Horns reared, grim mouth, deliberate pace,
You glide in silken silence where
The feast awaits your grace.

Strange partners, Snail! Then I, abed,
Consign the thick-darked vault to you,
Nor heed what sweetness night may shed
Nor moonshine's slumberous dew.

By Walter de la Mare
From: Collected Poems
Faber & Faber, 1979
ISBN 0-571-11382-6

AUGUST

Sympetrum
[dragonfly]

AUGUST

10th August, 1980

At the boundary of Little Stead overlooking the pond, a large bed of creeping thistle was alive with feeding tortoiseshell butterflies. Although a common species, few species of butterfly are richer in pattern and colour. The wings are bright russet contrasting with cream set in blackmarkings. For me this butterfly has an irresistible attraction. However, these jewels of the countryside lose their lustre in adverse weather conditions; their wings become torn and colours fade.

For the first time I saw a painted lady butterfly. This aptly named and exquisite insect is a delight to the eye. The wings are patterned dark brown in juxtaposition with a pinkish brown and splashes of white. Only too soon this offspring of a visitor from the Mediterranean vanished from my view. The painted lady usually reaches the southern parts of Britain in May and June. The female lays her eggs in June and July and the ensuing offspring emerge from July to October, after which they migrate to the south.

10th August, 1983

The last three weeks have been dry and sunny and today was no exception. The evening sky had all the grandeur of a William Turner sunset. The air was still and the landscape tinged with the soft colours of autumn. Farmers were already burning stubble, the noxious fumes drifting over the land. And yet the corn fields on either side of the main dyke remain unreaped. A field of potatoes displayed acres of motionless white flowerheads. The blue van of a patient fisherman lingered near the pond. At the eleventh hour swallows scooped their suppers on flickering wings.

I found the north dyke cleared of reedmace, the leaves and stems cast along the bank side to decay. The fruit of hawthorn and wild rose hung green as gooseberries, indian balsam, or policeman's helmet, was at it's best; the bright, green spear headed leaves contrasting with the sculptured form of the pinkish-mauve flowerheads. Honeybees were their constant visitors, even at this late hour, burrowing deeply into the delicate tubular blooms.

There were few sounds, most audible was "a little bit of bread and no cheese" with emphasis on "cheese" chirped by a yellow hammer. At a distance the staccato pop of shotguns from a clay pigeon shoot inter-mingled with the faint cries of playing children in the village.

With advancing darkness the solid shape of woodland became a low lying silhouette and the diminishing light gleamed as a reflection from the bristle of golden stubble. The first stage of autumn had started.

24th August, 1981

Visited the dykes for about an hour. I saw plenty of wall brown, meadow brown and peacock butterflies and was able to photograph them.

Fresh white marguerites were blooming freely and reedmace were well advanced with their tall, bright green, swordlike leaves gleaming in the sunlight. Banks of nettles supported colonies of the larvae of the small tortoiseshell butterfly. Even in the short time I spent I felt a renewed interest in looking at nature.

Autumn Hawkbit

THE OWL

Owl of the wildwood I:
Muffled in sleep I drowse,
Where no fierce sun in heaven
Can me arouse.

My haunt's a hollow
In a half-dead tree,
Whose strangled ivy
Shields and shelters me.

But when dark's starlight
Thrids my green domain,
My plumage trembles and stirs,
I wake again:

A spectral moon
Silvers the world I see;
Out of their day long lairs
Creep thievishly

Night's living things.
Then I,
Wafted away on soundless pinions
Fly;
Curdling her arches
With my hunting-cry:

A-hooh! a-hooh;
Four notes; and then,
Solemn, sepulchral, cold,
Four notes again,
The listening dingles
Of my woodland through:

A-hooh! A-hooh!
A-hooh!

W. de la Mare
Faber & Faber, 1979

Joseph
Doyle

Tawny owl

SEPTEMBER

Pods of Common Vetch

SEPTEMBER

6th September, 1984

My visit was fortuitous for the men from the waterboard had come to cut the herbage along the dykes. This was done by tractor which powered a cylinder cutter attached to an hydraulic arm. With the cutters angled, the steep sides of the dyke were trimmed with ease. One of the men I talked to was dressed in well-worn clothes and had a lined weatherbeaten face. He had a sense of humour and, seeing my camera, said "t'lad o'tractor ud like 'is photey tek'n" ! And I took it. He told me that soon the dykers would come to clear the water of reedmace.

12th September, 1981

Edna and I visited the dyke and the river for the pleasure of a walk. The fine sunny day produced a "skyscape" of cumulus clouds. Heavy showers had washed the lands and we wondered how butterflies, amongst other insects, had survived the beating raindrops.

We watched a magnificent specimen of the red admiral butterfly gliding with superb ease. This ability seems common with the larger butterflies. We saw the dyke being trimmed, and breathed in the heady scent of the freshly cut "pot pourri". Gone was the rich growth of wild grasses and flowers to be replaced by a "short back and sides". The vegetation had long since cast its seed ensuring a succession the following year.

13th September, 1981

I used by new macro coupler which permits greater close-ups in photography; I had no difficulty in filling the frame (or viewfinder) with a specimen of robin's pin cushion no more than three quarters of an inch in diameter. This cushion or gall, is formed by the activity of a gall wasp larvae living in the growing plant tissue.

This month marks a change in the colour of herbage. It is a change which ushers in Autumn. The cool greens of summer are transmuted to warm light browns. The tall, dense, corn and barley stalks in fields flanking the main dyke have gone. And with them the homes and feeding grounds of their summer residents; the harvest mouse, the hare, the redlegged partridge and pheasant. In the wake of the combine harvester lies a haze of pale golden stubble and, in the aftermath of summer, flocks of sparrow, feral pigeons and wood pigeons build their winter reserves from the gleanings.

My thoughts turn to harvest festivals and the colourful displays of fruit, vegetables and flowers. This is reflected in the countryside in places where the wild fruit is allowed to flourish and sustain wildlife. Sadly, too often, the encroachment of modern farming and urban development erodes this supply causing wild creatures to retreat, and we see how wildlife gardening in our urban areas can help redress the balance.

15th September, 1983

Today the clouds were brilliantly sunlit, casting strong, blue grey shadows on their undersides. This picture produced an exciting sensation in me.

The twitter of swallows reminded me of their impending migration to the shores of Africa. Above Little Steads, a kestrel quartered the stubble. The moorhen family on the pond quietly took cover amongst the reedmace at my approach. And here I saw flocks of sparrow feeding on hawthorn berries – and much less nervous of me than the menacing kestrel. I marvelled at their skilful flight as warning was given; in a group, as though rehearsed, they would sweep upward and dive into the cover of foliage. This manoeuvre demonstrated convincingly the sparrow's defence against predators.

Indian balsam was still in flower after a long season, now battered and windswept; also in bloom was clover and the deeply scented yarrow.

I had noticed a bird flying with rapid wing beats and could discern its black and white body; another characteristic was the long beak and by checking references at home I identified this as an oystercatcher. I wondered if the bird had found a local habitat. I understand that the oystercatcher, normally a bird of the seashore and estuary, is increasing its numbers inland.

As I returned I gazed at the flat land, taking in a slice at a time. The sun was incandescent; clouds formed a panorama of darkened shapes in random pattern; sunbeams split the clouds and created a dramatic effect of light and shade. This effect is not uncommon yet each occasion seems unique.

18th September, 1980

The pond is a wild life habitat in spite of its regular use by fishermen from a local angling club, and in spite of the abandoned newspaper, plastic bags, bottles and other debris left after a day's fishing. The countryside code says "leave no litter".

This spot harbours at least one family of mallards and more than one family of moorhens which have successfully adapted themselves to sharing their home with human incomers. This is not the case with the herons which visit; they prefer to fish in solitude and have to wait their opportunity. I have watched them soar away in spectacular flight well before I have reached the pond. A heron can climb quite rapidly and soon appears not much larger than a gull. The long neck retracts to complete the illusion.

Whilst fishing is in progress the resident birds seek refuge in the beds of common reeds around the margins, making only a rare appearance.

28th September, 1983

At Clough Dyke the cornfields were naked and spoke of the coming winter. Light September mists rendered soft tones to the distant landscapes, whilst colours in the foreground were warmed by weak sunlight and I felt compelled to photograph the scene.

In the sugar beet fields, where earlier I had seen lapwings nesting, a sugar beet harvesting machine rested and the dark ash of burnt stubble formed wavy pathways through the cornfield.

I found a specimen of the quite common sympetrum dragonfly basking on a tile by the roadside. This was the first one I had seen here and it was most content to fly around and then return to its platform for warmth and to 'pose' for a photograph. True to his species of darter dragonflies, his circuits were swift. This species can also be found at some distance from it's watery habitat, as on another occasion, I discovered one resting on our clothes line.

Adjoining field - burnt stubble

ODE TO AUTUMN

Where are the songs of Spring? Aye, where are they?
Think not of them, – thou hast thy music too,
While barred clouds bloom the soft dying day,
And touch the stubble-plains with rosy hue;
Then in a wailful choir the small gnats mourn
Among the river-sallows, borne aloft
Or sinking as the light winds lives or dies;
And full grown lambs loud bleat from hillybourn;
Hedge-crickets sing; and now with treble soft
The redbreast whistles from a garden-croft;
And gathering swallows twitter in the skies.

From the poem "To Autumn"
By John Keats.
From The Oxford Library of English Poetry Vol. 2

OCTOBER

After
the plough

OCTOBER

4th October, 1983

Little Steads to the south was alive with tractors. Three of them worked as a team preparing the land for next year's crop. The lead tractor sliced the soil with three brightly polished plough shares. A few yards behind, a second tractor pulled a cultivator breaking up the earth turned by the plough. The last of the trio pulled a harrow which combed the surface to a fine tilth. I was impressed by the efficiency of this method which I had never seen before. A fourth machine towed a trailer laden with sacks of grain for sowing.

With the ritual of farming there is a close relationship between agriculture and wildlife. And around the disturbed soil at Little Steads a flock of black-headed gulls and lapwings wheeled and alighted to snatch up the riches. This is an example of mutual help which is of great benefit to both farmer and bird. Beyond this is the spectacle of activity which is a pleasure to watch.

4th October, 1983

This evening presented a sky of contrasting clouds set against a blue sky; they were lit by a sun positioned nearer to the horizon at this time of year. The sunlit crests of the

Ash keys

swollen cumulus clouds appeared as a snow capped mountain range, whilst high above spread a formal pattern of mackerel clouds.

The tall, dry, grass stalks bent with the wind and sturdy hawthorns shook under it's pressure; snug within the tangle of sharp twigs, a familiar colony of sparrows sheltered.

From the reeds of the pond a family of moorhens emerged, one by one, unperturbed by my presence. Through binoculars I could clearly see the white flashes on the rump and the sharply pointed wing tips above their backs. I had the pleasure of watching a solitary adult moorhen carrying out it's ablutions in the seclusion and safety of a reed bed. The bird was able to reach all parts of it's body (whilst preening) with the exception of the head and upper parts of the neck. The cleaning is achieved with ease and grace. Like most waterbirds the moorhen also waterproofs its feathers by rolling the sides and back of its head over a gland on the lowest part of the back. The gland contains an oily secretion which the bird then transfers from its head to its body and wing feathers.

12th October, 1985

A good dry month with a fair amount of sun. At the pond a flock of fieldfare chattered harshly amongst the hawthorns as they took their fill of the berries hanging in abundance; they were accompanied by yellowhammers who shared this feast. Unfortunately, the birds moved away nervously at my approach, and I lost the opportunity to study their colouring properly

Summer had gone, leaving the landscape bathed in the warm colour of autumn.

NOVEMBER

Kindling (Marsh Lane) 1987

NOVEMBER

28th November, 1982

Along the trim banks of the north dyke I found small heaps of fine soil thrown up by a mole. Among the soil lay small clusters of milk white eggs, 1mm in diameter. They were strange to me, and I wondered if these were slug or snail eggs.

Many of the rose hips had been eaten, hinting that the migrating fieldfares and red-wing were amongst us. The trilling notes of a flock of skylarks were audible, and further afield could be heard the sharper notes of finches and the harsh cry of magpies. Crows and rooks were very active and large flocks moved between feeding grounds and roosts. The accent now is on continuous feeding from the seeds and insects of summer to provide sustenance against the bite of winter.

Ivy fruit

27th November, 1983

Felt I must visit the dyke after a long absence. The fields were covered with a haze of leaf green; a resurrection, in the form of winter corn, with it's promise of summer harvest. An anxious cock pheasant hurried across a field for cover. His home as a chick would have been in captivity for these pheasants, and partridges, are bred for the table; I could not help thinking of his short life without a tinge of regret.

The banks of Clough Dyke were smooth and well defined; the water wound its silent way towards the pond. A peaceful scene, and it is this peace and the everchanging face of the countryside which beckons me to return. Wheeling and weaving like fairground dodgems, clouds of midges played above the dyke. Near the water level I counted approximately a dozen holes serving the entrance and exit of the water vole community. So secretive are these small animals that I have only seen one- swimming across the dyke. "Ratty" as he is named by Kenneth Grahame in his book "Wind in the Willows", is strictly incorrect, as he is not a water rat, although so named. The vole is an endearing creature in its habits and appearance. A furry body looking plump when sitting, is rather surprisingly elongated when swimming. He has a broad head with small ears and eyes; so short sighted as to be deserving of spectacles! However, what a vole lacks in vision is compensated for by an ability to scent danger and rely on hearing. He is timid, and wisely so in a world crowded with enemies. In the water he is prey to the pike and trout; on land he is attacked by the weasel, stoat and fox; from the air the threat comes from owl and hawk. In this area it is the short-eared owl, the tawny owl and kestrel which comb the dykes for food. The vole limits his boundary to approximately 100 yards from his system of tunnels in the river bank and he marks the area with a secretion from his flanks – so warning other voles of his territory. It has been discovered that he can be fond of apples, although his normal diet consists of cropping grass, creating a "lawn".

In favourable conditions a vole pair are capable of producing a few families in one year and this redresses the balance when we know that the adult vole is unlikely to survive more than one year. We also know that in years when voles are prolific, so the number of owls and their offspring increase. The vole uses certain spots as a toilet, where its droppings are easily recognised by the naturalist. The smell of a dried droppings is surprisingly pleasant of herbs.

Voles are attracted to apples and to test this theory one day I placed slices of apple near their burrows. Sure enough the apple disappeared – when I was absent!

water vole

DECEMBER

LEISURE

What is this life if, full of care,
We have no time to stand and stare.

No time to stand beneath the boughs
And stare as long as sheep or cows.

No time to see, when woods we pass,
Where squirrels hide their nuts in grass

No time to see, in broad daylight,
Streams full of stars like skies at night.

No time to turn at Beauty's glance,
And watch her feet, how they can dance.

No time to wait till her mouth can
Enrich that smile her eyes began.

A poor life this if, full of care,
We have no time to stand and stare.

By W.H. Davies
From The Collins Book of Best-Loved Verse
Chosen by Charles Osborne
Published 1986

DECEMBER

12th December, 1983

A layer of snow, but a good day, when the whiteness combined with a flawless blue sky. A kestrel above me was bathed in reflected light, seeming ethereal, born of air and light. This is a moment of magic for the walker in the countryside. Such a landscape breathes serenity and quietness peculiar to a fall of snow. Footprints of animals are easily detected and I found those of the hare in many places. I was interested in groups of smaller prints with a gap of roughly two feet between; were these made by a stoat or weasel?

By the frozen grey pond, a fieldfare chivvied a blackbird whilst both were feeding from rosehips. As I gazed at the pond, I realised that the heron would be restricted to fishing from the shallows of the river. I thought also of the hare, which nibbles away at any gleanings of sugar beet, now that its supply of grass is in short supply. How vulnerable the brown hare looks, a dark silhouette against white. We see how well animals are adapted to their surroundings as in the case of the mountain hare who grows a white winter coat.

Pond, Wistow Clough

FULL STOP

My jottings and illustrations were started in 1980, and finished in 1988 during a time when I could devote more time to painting. I visited Wistow Clough approximately 100 times. I call them jottings because that is how my writing began and painting followed as a pleasure and I did not think of publishing them as a book until recently; this was in part, due to the support and encouragement of my family.

Since the last entry in 1988, the cycle of wildlife activities continues to thrive and are there to enjoy.

SONNET

The world is too much with us; late and soon,
Getting and spending, we lay waste our powers;
Little we see in Nature that is ours;
We have given our hearts away, a sordid boon!
This sea that bares her bosom to the moon,
The winds that will be howling at all hours
And are up-gathered now like sleeping flowers,
For this, for everything, we are out of tune;
It moves us not. Great God! I'd rather be
A Pagan suckled in a creed outworn,
So might I, standing on this pleasant lea,
Have glimpses that would make me less forlorn;
Have sight of Proteus rising from the sea;
Or hear old Triton blow his wreathed horn.

By W. Wordsworth 1770-1850
From Palgrave's Golden Treasury
Oxford University Press

PLANTS FOUND ON THE DYKE, NEAR THE POND AND RIVERBANK

Black Medick
Birdsfoot Trefoil
Burdock
Bramble
Bittersweet (Wood Nightshade)
Brown Knapweed
Buttercup
Bedstraw
Cowslip
Cow Parsley
Creeping Thistle
Coltsfoot
Common Vetch
Convolvulus
Common Meadow Rue
Catear
Crosswort
Chickweed
Creeping Cinquefoil
Camomile
Cranesbill
Dead Nettle, White
Daisy
Dandelion
Dock
Dog Rose
Daffodil
Ground Ivy
Giant Bellflower
Germander Speedwell
Ground Elder
Greater Burnet Saxifrage
Goosegrass
Great Willow Herb
Hogweed
Horsetail
Hemlock
Hedgewoundwort

Hairy Tare
Indian Balsom
Lesser Celandine
Lords and Ladies
Meadowsweet
Mustard Garlic
Marsh Horsetail
Marsh Pea
Meadow Cranesbill
Marsh Thistle
Mouse-ear Chickweed
Ox-eye Daisy
Pineapple Weed
(Pineapple Mayweed)
Ribwort
Rape or Cole
Ribwort Plantain
Red Clover
Red Shank Persicaria
Red Veined Dock
Ragwort
Stinging Nettle
Silver Weed
Scented Mayweed
Stitchwort
St John's Wort
Snowdrop
Tansy
Tufted Vetch
Wood Speedwell
White Clover
Water Forget-me-not
Wall Lettuce
Wild Angelica
Yellow Meadow Vetchling
Yarrow
Yellow Vetch
Zigzag Clover

PLANTS ASSOCIATED WITH WATER

Water Burr-weed
Brooklime
Bulrush (Reedmace)
Celery leaved Crowfoot
Common Reed

Floating Pond Weed
Polygonium Amphibian
Water Cress
Water Forget-me-not
Water Plantain

TREES, SHRUBS AND BUSHES

Alder
Ash
Buckthorn
Elderberry
Hawthorn

Maple
Oak
Poplar
Willow

BUTTERFLIES AND MOTHS

Common Blue
Cinnabar
Hedgebrown
Large White
Meadow Brown
Orangetip

Painted Lady
Peacock
Small Tortoiseshell
Skipper
Wall Brown
Cream Wave Moth

BIRDS SIGHTED AT WISTOW CLOUGH

Fields and hedgerows

Blackbird
Blue Tit
Carrion Crow
Corn Bunting

Cuckoo (migrant)
Feral Pigeon
Fieldfare (migrant)
Goldfinch

Greenfinch
House Sparrow
Kestrel
Lapwing
Magpie
Pheasant
Reed Bunting
Red-legged Partridge
Redwing (migrant)
Robin
Rook

Skylark
Short-eared Owl
Sparrowhawk
Starling
Swallow (migrant)
Tawny Owl
Thrush
Tree Sparrow
Wood Pigeon
Yellow Hammer
Wren

Birds associated with water

Black-headed gull
Grey Wagtail
Heron
Mallard

Moorhen
Oyster Catcher
Coot

REFERENCES

The Lower Vale of Wharfe and York by Edmund Bogg, 3 Wade Street, Leeds.

Wild Flowers of Britain by Roger Phillips. Book Club Associates, London. CN 4479.

The Concise British Flora in Colour by W. Kebble Martin. Published by Sphere. ISBN 0 7221 0503 7.

The Oxford Book of Insects by John Burton. Published by Oxford University Press. ISBN 0 19 910005 5.

Book of the British Countryside. Published by Drive Publications. Hodder and Stoughton. ISBN 0 903356 11 2.

The Reader's Digest Book of British Birds. Published by Drive Publications. Collins Publishers.

The Amateur Naturalist by Gerald Durrell. Published by Hamish Hamilton, London. ISBN 0 241 10841 1.

A Field Guide to the Nests, Eggs and Nestlings of British and European Birds by Colin Harrison. Published by Collins. ISBN 0 00 219335 3.

Field Guide to the Water Life of Britain. Published by the Reader's Digest Association Ltd. ISBN 0 276 36008 7.

The Observer's Book of Pond Life by John Clegg. Published by Frederick Warne, London. ISBN 0 7232 1608 8.

The Observer's Book of Wild Flowers by Francis Rose. Published by Frederick Warne Ltd. ISBN 0 7232 1584 7.

Carl Linnaeus Travels. Nature Classics by David Black. Felix Gluck Press Ltd.

Mammals of the British Isles by L. Harrison Mathews. Published by Collins.

The Collected Poems of Walter De La Mare. Published by Faber and Faber 1979.

The Wood is Sweet – John Clare chosen by David Powell. Published by Bodley Head 1971.

The Golden Treasury by F.T. Palgrave. Selected by John Press 1964.

The Collins Book of Best-Loved Verse 1987.

ILLUSTRATIONS

ALWYN JOSEPH DOYLE

Alwyn Joseph Doyle lives in Brayton, Selby.
Born in Horbury, Wakefield.
Former student of the Leeds College of Art
and the Royal College, London.
Former teacher of Art at Read School near
Selby and latterly, Selby College – Principal
part-time lecturer.
Former Director of Landscape and Flower
Painting at Grantley Hall Residential College.
Co-director of Art, Selby Festival, 1966.
Exhibited work in Yorkshire and the Royal
Academy.
Friend of the Royal Academy and Beverley
Art Gallery.
Exhibiting Member of Leeds Fine Art Club.
Membership of the York Art Workers
Association, the National Art Collection Fund,
Yorkshire Wildlife Trust and The National
Trust and The Saturday People, Swathmore
Institute, Leeds.

At present he is concentrating on printmaking
and has a wide-ranging interest in the Arts
and Countryside.

The drawing is of a hand carved Chinese marble
seal with my name Joseph translated into
Chinese. The paintings printed with my name
in Chinese were used in an early exhibition when
I decided to use the seal because of its aesthetic
qualities and where there was space, and
since abandoned.

104